Revised Edition

Collins

EXCURSIONS

A course in Environmental Studies

1

Series Editor
Abira Das

Student + Teacher			Teacher-only	
a animations	**ia** activities	**g** games	**lp** lesson plans	**tn** teacher's notes
ilt instructor-led tutorials	**w** worksheets	**v** videos	**w** worksheets	**ak** answer keys
	audio			

Preface

***Excursions* Revised Edition** is a comprehensive course in Environmental Studies and Social Studies for young learners. This series for classes 1 to 8 is aligned to the National Education Policy, 2020. Following the curriculum, the series offers a course in Environmental Studies for classes 1 and 2, integrated Social Studies for classes 3, 4 and 5 and separate Geography and History and Civics courses for classes 6, 7 and 8. The series offers features that focus on essential skills to assist learners achieve holistic learning through a multidisciplinary approach.

Environmental Studies is the interdisciplinary search for knowledge and understanding of the natural (physical and biotic) systems and of their dynamic interactions with humankind. Thus, its scope covers areas of both Science and Social Studies in an integrated manner. Learners are guided to look at the environment in a holistic way and see the underlying unity in the physical and social environment.

In line with the latest syllabus, the series follows a thematic and structured approach. The course material provides activities for cross-curricular linkages to connect learning across subject areas. Based on an interactive pedagogy, the books promote learning through inferential and experiential tasks and stimulating content. The series provides ample scope for the learners to observe, reflect, hone their thinking skills and develop e ffective communication skills.

About the series editor

Abira Das, has over 22 years of experience in teaching with Agrasain Group of Institutions. Her passion for teaching is innate and in her tenure as an educator, she has worked in the capacity of a teacher, an academic coordinator, a CEO and a principal. Currently, she is the principal in the prestigious Agrasain Boys' School, Kolkata.

Key Features

Varied key features in the series hone learning skills.

- **Learning** – Let's learn about, Key terms, Timeline, In a Nutshell
- **Extended learning and explanation** – Reflect, FactPedia, Figure Out, Weblinks
- **Observation and application** – DIY, Green Earth, World Connect, Geo Connect, Case Study
- **Problem solving and analytical thinking** – Think Box, Life Skills and Values, Picture Study
- **Creativity and happiness** – Enjoy, Game
- **Multidisciplinary and holistic learning** – Across the Boundary, Snap Recap
- **Assessment and practice** – Workout, Test Yourself, Outline maps

The comprehensive teacher's resource materials are aimed at facilitating teaching and assessment. Feedback and suggestions to improve the course further are welcome.

Key Features

Excursions Revised Edition offers features that focus on essential skills to assist learners achieve holistic learning through a multidisciplinary approach. In so doing, the series is aligned with the guidelines given in the National Education Policy, 2020.

Learning

Let's learn about...

- ourselves.
- our likes and dislikes.
- our hobbies.

Outlines the learning outcomes of the chapter

Key Terms

- friends
- likes
- dislikes
- hobbies
- identity card

Lists the important terms used in the chapter

In a Nutshell

- Friends study and play together and help one another.
- Different people have different likes and dislikes.

Gives a ready reckoner to reinforce learning

Extended Learning and Application

Reflect

Identify these people who help us.

Includes warm-up tasks to initiate the learners into the topic and relate to it

FactPedia

A **tepee** is a tall tent shaped like a cone.

Provides interesting titbits of information

Figure Out

Read the poem. Name the part of our body used to do these activities.

I can hear the birds sing,
the dogs bark, the cat meow,
I can hear the phone ring,
I can hear you!

Hones referencing and research skills through small tasks

Observation and Application

Green Earth

Paper is made from trees. We should reuse old wrapping paper for gifts to save trees.

Sensitizes learners towards conservation of the environment

DIY

Look at these pictures. Write whether you see them at night or during the day.

Provides application-based activities for experiential learning

Problem-solving and Analytical Tasks

Think Box

1. I met a creature on the road;
On its back it had a load.
It wasn't an ass and it wasn't a cow,
Though two horns grew on its brow.
....

(HOTS) Facilitates out-of-the-box thinking for curious minds

Life Skills and Values

What do you do with your old clothes? Tick the correct option.

1. Give them to a younger child in the family. ☐
2. Put them in a garbage bag to throw. ☐
3. Ask your parents to give them to charity. ☐
4. Give it to your helpers or their children. ☐

Provides real-life situations to skill learners to excel in life

Creativity and Happiness

Enjoy

Make a model of the solar system

You will need yellow craft paper, eight sticks of different lengths and eight buttons of different colours.

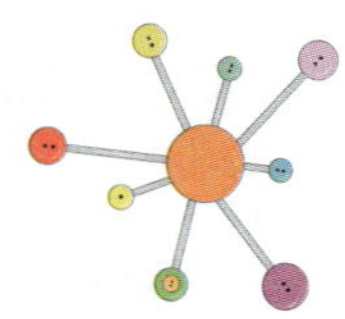

Addresses well-being and happiness of the students through creative and fun tasks

Multidisciplinary and Holistic Learning

Across the Boundary 2

Look at the pictures. Write whether you see, hear, touch, smell or taste while doing these activities. One has been done for you.

1. I see 2. .... 3. .... 4. ....

Provides varied activities for multidisciplinary learning

Assessment and Practice

Workout

A. Circle the correct answers.

1. Friends play (together/alone).
2. Friends (sleep/eat) together in school.
3. Hobbies are activities that we like to do during (school hours/our free time).

To facilitate assessment

Test Yourself I

A. Write T for true and F for false.

1. We need food to live, grow and stay healthy. ....
2. *Kuchcha* houses are made of cement and bricks. ....
3. We have three meals in a day—breakfast, lunch and dinner. ....
4. Clothes cover our body and keep us warm. ....

B. Match the columns.

	Column A	Column B
1.	hobby	a. outdoor game
2.	breathe	b. mud and straw
3.	siblings	c. done in free time
4.	hopscotch	d. nose
5.	*kuchcha* house	e. brothers and sisters

To facilitate evaluation

Contents

1 This Is Me

Let's learn about...

- ourselves.
- our likes and dislikes.
- our hobbies.

Key Terms

- friends
- likes
- dislikes
- hobbies
- identity card

Reflect

Tick the activities you like to do.

1.  ☐
2.  ☐
3.  ☐
4.  ☐
5.  ☐

Hi, my name is Supriya. I am five years old. I love to play the drums.

I go to school every day. I have many friends in school. We do many things together.

Playing drums

Tick the things that you do with your friends.

- Play ☐
- Study ☐
- Eat ☐

Identity Cards

Have you seen children wearing cards in school? These are called identity cards. The card tells us a few things about the person wearing it, such as, his or her name, class and birthday.

DIY

Write about yourself and paste your photograph to complete the identity card.

Name: ....

Mothers' name: ....

Fathers' name: ....

Date of birth: ....

Phone number: ....

Address: ....

....

Paste your photograph here

Things I like

FactPedia
All of us like different things. This makes us special.

Ankit is Supriya's best friend. While Supriya learns to play music at school, Ankit goes to the library. He does not like playing music, but likes reading books. Different people have different likes and dislikes.

A hobby is an activity, we enjoy doing the most during our free time. People have different hobbies. Painting, cycling, writing and reading are some hobbies.

Painting

Cycling

Reading

Green Earth
Gardening is the hobby of growing plants and taking care of them. Plants make the air clean.

Write the name of two activities that you like to do in your free time.

....

In a Nutshell

- Friends study and play together and help one another.
- Different people have different likes and dislikes.
- A hobby is an activity, we enjoy doing the most during our free time.

Workout

A. Circle the correct answers.

1. Friends play (together/alone).
2. Friends (sleep/eat) together in school.
3. Hobbies are activities that we like to do during (school hours/our free time).
4. Different people have (similar/different) likes and dislikes.

B. Colour the fish that show the hobbies that interest you.

C. Write Yes or No.

1. I wear glasses. ....
2. I have a bicycle. ....
3. I have a hobby. ....
4. I have curly hair. ....

D. Answer these questions.

1. What is an identity card?

....

....

2. What is a hobby?

....

....

3. Which is your favourite cartoon show?

....

....

Think Box

Discuss your hobbies with your friends. Does anyone like doing the same activities as you? Find out which hobby gets the most number of likes.

Life Skills and Values

We all have some interests. Some of us are good at writing and some of us are good at dancing. Sometimes we are not good at some activities. Now complete this table.

I think I am good at	
My family members are	
My favourite thing is	
Sometimes I need help with	
When I grow up, I want to be	

Enjoy

A. Make a **Me** poster.

Dip your hand in a plate of paint. Press your hand on a sheet of paper to get your handprint. Write your name on it and pin it up on a board.

B. Colour these pictures.

2 All About Me

Let's learn about...

- the parts of our body.
- our sense organs.
- taking care of our body.

Key Terms

- parts of the body
- sense organs
- senses

Reflect

Do these activities and write which part of your body you used.

- Snap your fingers ....
- Listen to the birds sing ....
- Eat delicious cookies ....

Our body helps us to do many things. It has many parts. Each part of the body is important.

Parts of Our Body

Each part of our body is useful. We use different parts of our body to do different actions. We breathe through our nose. We stand, walk, run and jump with the help of our legs.

We use our arms and hands to hold, eat, write, draw and many more actions.

Look at the picture and read aloud the names of the parts of the body along with your teacher.

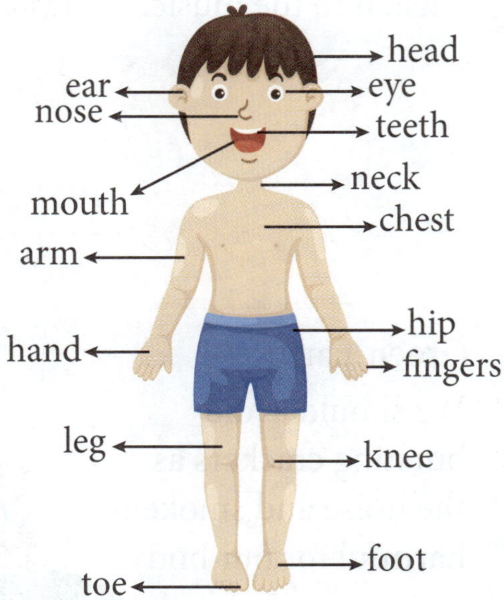

Parts of our body

breathe: to take air inside your body and send it out again

Sense Organs

We can see, hear, taste, smell and feel. These are our five senses.

Our eyes, ears, tongue, nose and skin help us do these things. These are called sense organs. All sense organs help us know and feel the world around us.

sense organs

DIY

Write the names of the parts of the body that we use to do these activities.

1. 
We use our .... to listen to the music.

2. 
We use our .... to taste the ice cream.

3. 
We use our .... to play football.

4. 
We use our .... to hold the kitten.

Figure Out

Read the poem. Name the part of our body used to do these activities.

I can hear the birds sing,
the dogs bark, the cat meow,
I can hear the phone ring,
I can hear you!

....

Green Earth

We should avoid bursting crackers as the noise and smoke is harmful for our body.

sense organs: parts of the body that help us see, hear, taste, smell, and touch

Taking Care of the Body

To keep ourselves fit, we should take care of our body. We must:

- wash our hands regularly.
- eat healthy food.
- take a bath everyday.
- drink plenty of water.
- exercise and play daily.

Wash your hands often

FactPedia
Our arms and legs together are known as our limbs.

In a Nutshell

- Our body helps us to do many things.
- Each part of our body is useful.
- We have five sense organs.
- We should keep ourselves fit.

Sing this rhyme to a tune.

My hands are for clapping.
My arms hug tight.
My fingers snap,
or can turn out the light.
My legs are for jumping.
My eyes help me see,
This is my body
and I love all of me.

Workout

A. Which of these activities can you do? Colour the boxes with green colour.

1. Leap like a frog ☐
2. Write with your left hand ☐
3. Fly like a bird ☐
4. Stand on one foot till the count of 20 ☐

B. Circle the things that you do with the help of your legs.

write walk hold jump sing run

regularly: to do an activity every day

C. Underline the correct answers.

1. I am just above your neck. (head/shoulders)
2. I am just above your feet. (knees/chest)
3. I am just below your eyes. (mouth/ears)
4. I am at the end of your arm. (hand/elbow)

D. Answer these questions.

1. How do our hands help us?

   ....

   ....

2. Write two things that our legs help us do.

   ....

   ....

3. How do sense organs help us?

   ....

   ....

4. Write two things we should do to keep ourselves fit.

   ....

   ....

Think Box

Observe a bird, dog, cat and an ant. Think and say which part of the body these animals use to move.

Life Skills and Values

A. Our body is very important to us. We should take care of our body. Exercise keeps us fit and active. List five exercises that you do daily at school to stay fit.

B. In groups of five, write a short poem on parts of your body. You can write about what you do with the different parts of your body. For example, we tap with our feet and count on our fingers.

Enjoy

Make your own clay model.

You will need modelling sticks and clay.

- Make balls of different shapes and sizes.
- Make a pear-shaped body with the bigger ball of clay.
- Make the arms, legs, head, hands and feet using the clay.
- Fix them to the body with the modelling sticks.
- Use old buttons as eyes.
- Keep the model out in the sun to dry.
- Your clay model is ready.

3 Our Family

Let's learn about...

- types of families.
- family members.
- friends and neighbours.

Key Terms

- family
- joint family
- cousins
- grandparents
- parents
- uncle
- small family
- sibling
- aunt

Reflect

Look at these pictures. What do you see in them? Do animals also have families?

We all live in a family. A family is a group of people living together. A mother, father and their children make a family. Our parents are our mother and father. Our sisters and brothers are called siblings. Family members sometimes look like one another. Parents look after their children. Children also help their parents.

Types of Families

Small family

Families are of different types. Aadila lives with her father, mother and her brother. She stays in a small family. Parents and children living together make a small family which is also called a nuclear family.

FactPedia

A one-parent family is a family that consists of only one parent and his or her children living together.

Abhinav lives with his father, mother and grandparents. He lives in a large family. Sometimes, uncles, aunts with their children also live in large families. This type of family is called a joint family. Family members love and care for one another. They also help one another.

Joint family

Give one way in which you help your family.

....

FactPedia
All family members share the same last name. This is called a surname.

Family Relations

Grandparents, uncles, aunts and our cousins are our relatives. You know that our parent's father is our grandfather and their mother is our grandmother. The brothers and sisters of our parents are our uncles and aunts. Their children are our cousins. Family relations are shown on a family tree. Let us look at Vishal's family tree.

Vishal's family tree

DIY

Tick the activities that show family members care for each other.

1.  ☐

2.  ☐

3.  ☐

4.  ☐

Friends and Neighbours

Our neighbours are the people who live near our home. They help us in times of need. We should help them too. Together, we take care of our elders. Our neighbour's children are our friends. Sometimes, we go to the same school. We all play together and have fun.

Helping the elderly

Playing with your pet

Bhavya plays with her dog, Sheru. Animals who live with us are our pets. They are a part of our family. Our helpers are also part of our family. We must take care of both of them.

Green Earth

We should take care of the animals that do not live with us too.

In a Nutshell

- A family is a group of people living together.
- A family can be small or large.
- Family members love and care for one another.
- Grandparents, uncles, aunts and our cousins are our relatives.
- Our neighbours are the people who live near us.
- We must take care of both, our pets and our helpers.

Workout

A. Write True or False.

1. Members of a family do not look like one another. ....

2. Family members love one another. ....

3. Family members always live together. ....

4. A family takes care of the elderly members. ....

B. Match the following.

1.	Your father's sister is your	a.	grandchild
2.	Your mother's mother is your	b.	cousin
3.	You are your grandfather's	c.	grandmother
4.	Your uncle's daughter is your	d.	aunt

C. Answer these questions.

1. Do you live in a small or a large family?

....

....

2. Write one way in which you take care of your pets, if any, and your helpers?

....

....

3. Write two fun activities that you do with your friends.

....

....

Think Box

Who does these for you in your family?

1. Buys you things ....

2. Cleans the house ....

3. Helps you do homework ....

4. Cooks food ....

Life Skills and Values

Write your parents' mobile numbers and your home address in your diary.

1. Mother's number ....
2. Father's number ....
3. Home address ....

Enjoy

A. Make your own family album

You need: notebook, glue, markers, crayons, pencils, photos of family members, family photo

Collect the pictures of your family members. Paste their photos on a paper and write their names below it. You can make a colourful frame for the photo using crayons. On the last page of the photo album, draw your family tree. Stick the family photo on the cover of the album.

B. Make a My Family poster.

You will need ice cream sticks. Draw the faces of your family members on these sticks. Paste the sticks on a paper and pin it up.

Across the Boundary 1

Look at the family tree given here. Draw or paste the pictures of your grandparents, parents, siblings and pet, if any.

Now, write the names of your family members.

4 Fun With Family

Let's learn about...

- activities we do with our families.
- how family members help each other.

Key Terms

- festivals
- holidays
- sharing
- caring
- celebrations
- fun

Reflect

Complete the names of these family members.

1. F _ T H _ R
2. G R _ N _ M _ T H _ _
3. M _ T _ E _
4. S I _ _ _ R

Family members have fun together. Families celebrate festivals and holidays in different ways.

Fun During Festivals

Maria and John are very happy. It is Christmas and they are going to decorate the Christmas tree. They get Christmas gifts and their aunt bakes a cake. They enjoy a special dinner with their cousins. We celebrate festivals with our relatives, make special food and exchange gifts.

Celebrating Christmas

Green Earth

Paper is made from trees. We should reuse old wrapping paper for gifts to save trees.

Fun During Holidays

We all have fun with our families. We celebrate holidays and birthdays with our family members.

celebrate: do something special for an event or a day; decorate: make something look nice

We get together to meet our relatives and spend time with them. We usually spend long summer vacations with our grandparents.

Families also go on picnics and trips during holidays and have fun.

FactPedia
Raksha Bandhan is a festival that brothers and sisters celebrate together.

Name three activities that you do with your brothers, sisters and cousins.

....

Sharing and Caring

We must care for our family and share things with them. Sharing is caring. We ask our family members for help. Often we take help from our elder siblings or cousins to complete our school projects. We like it when our grandparents read out stories for us. We enjoy playing games like hopscotch, cricket or carom with our cousins. We care for our parents and grandparents.

Helping cousin in her work

Figure Out
Do you play games inside your house? Find out the names of three such games.

DIY

Imagine you have to go for a family picnic soon. Plan for it and list things you would be required to carry for the outing.

1. Clothes ....
2. Games ....
3. Food items ....
4. Drinks ....
5. Camera/umbrella/hat ....
6. Others ....

vacation: a period of the year when schools and colleges are closed; picnic: when we pack our food and go out to eat it at a different place; trip: going to a place for a few days to have fun hopscotch: a children's game played on a pattern of squares marked on the ground

In a Nutshell

- We celebrate festivals and birthdays with family members.
- Family members go out and spend time together.
- Family members help one another.
- Family members play games and have fun together.

Workout

A. Colour the activities that you like to do with your family in green colour.

Eat dinner | Play snakes and ladders | Do homework | Go for shopping

Ride a bicycle | Read | Dance

B. Underline the correct answers.

1. We celebrate festivals with our family and (classmates/neighbours).
2. We (should/should not) help our family members.
3. We go out for picnics with our families to have (fun/air).
4. We must (share/not share) our things with our siblings and cousins.
5. We have a feast with family and friends (every day/on festivals).

C. Answer these questions.

1. How do you spend time with your family members?

....

....

2. Write two ways in which you help your family members.

....

....

3. Name two games you like to play with your siblings and cousins.

....

....

D. Help Tina and Varun reach home.

Think Box

Some of us have grandparents in our homes or they come for short visits. How will you take care of your grandparents? Write two ways in which you will spend time with them.

Life Skills and Values

Answer this family quiz.

1. I have .... members in my family.
2. I have .... brother/s .... sister/s and .... cousin/s in my family.
3. I celebrate my birthday on .... with my family.
4. Me and my family decorate the house on .... (name of the festival).
5. I visited .... (name of the place) with my parents during my last summer vacation.

Enjoy

A. Make a greeting card to wish your parents on a festival.

Take a coloured sheet of paper and fold it into half. Draw a picture of the festival on the outside. Use colours to decorate it. Open the folded sheet and write a greeting inside. Put it in an envelope and give it to your parents.

B. Write this prayer on a piece of coloured paper and put it up in your room.

I have a family, nice and happy.
Sharing and caring for everybody.
We like to be merry and stay healthy.
God bless my family!

5 Food We Eat

Let's learn about...

- why do we need food.
- where we get food from.
- what healthy food is.
- cooked and uncooked food.

Key Terms

- healthy food
- breakfast
- lunch
- junk food
- dinner

Reflect

Name these food items.

1. ....   2. ....   3. ....

What is food?

Food is what people and animals eat. We need food to live and grow. It helps us to stay healthy and strong.

FactPedia
Water is an important part of food.

Food We Eat

Food gives us energy that we need to work and play. We eat different kinds of food items. These are fruits, vegetables, grains, meat and milk products.

We get our food from plants and animals. Plants provide us with fruits and vegetables. We get meat, eggs and milk from animals.

energy: strength to do any activity; milk products: food made from milk

DIY

Match the pictures of food items with their names.

1. 

2. 

3. 

4. 

- meat and fish
- grains
- vegetable and fruits
- milk products

Meals of the day

We should eat food regularly and on time. The three main meals of a day are breakfast, lunch and dinner. Breakfast in the morning is the most important meal of the day.

We eat breakfast in the morning.

We eat lunch in the afternoon.

We eat dinner at night.

Cooked and uncooked food

We eat food in both cooked and uncooked forms. Some food items can be eaten raw, that is, without cooking. Vegetables like, cucumber, carrot and tomato can be eaten raw in salads. Fruits are also eaten raw.

Uncooked food

Green Earth

One can grow vegetables at home by planting their seeds in a potted plant.

meal: the food served and eaten

We cook some food items to make them soft and tasty. Pulses, cereals, eggs and meat are eaten in their cooked form.

Food cooked during festivals

During festivals we cook many special dishes. We make traditional dishes, such as, *kheer*, *sewiyan*, pudding and we also eat sweets. Food like biryani and meals like *sadhya* are also cooked during festivals.

Kheer

Gujiya

Sadhya

Biryani

Pudding

Food for different people

Sometimes, different food items are made for different people. Do you know when babies start eating food, special soft food is given to them? This food helps the babies to grow. Elders and old people eat food which gives them energy and keeps their body strong. When we fall sick, we eat food that will make us healthy again.

Baby food

Food for sick

Healthy Food

Food, such as, fresh fruits and vegetables, eggs, milk and dal are healthy food. These food items give us energy and helps us grow. Food, such as, burgers, potato chips, pizzas and ice creams are unhealthy food. They are also called junk food and can make us sick. We should not eat them very often.

Unhealthy food

Healthy eating habits

- We must always eat fresh, covered and healthy food. If we do not eat fresh food, we can fall sick.
- We must drink a lot of water.

junk food: food that is unhealthy and easily prepared

- We must avoid eating too much of junk food.
- We should take our food slowly and chew it properly.
- We must not talk when we have food in our mouth.
- We should never waste food.

Figure Out

Which part of the body do you use to chew food?

In a Nutshell

- Food gives us energy to live, grow, work and play.
- We have three meals in a day—breakfast, lunch and dinner.
- We should eat healthy food.
- We eat special food during festivals.

Workout

A. Write R for uncooked and C for cooked for the food items given here.

1. Curd .... 2. Pulses ....
3. Chicken .... 4. Mango ....
5. Cucumber .... 6. Rice........................
7. Potatoes .... 8. Eggs ....

B. Write H for healthy food and U for unhealthy food.

1. 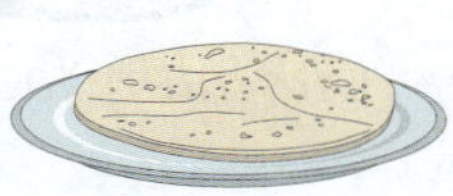 ☐

2. 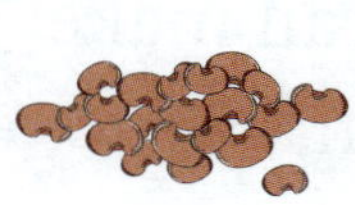 ☐

3.  ☐

4.  ☐

5.  ☐

6. 

☐

7.  ☐

8.  ☐

C. Answer these questions.

1. How does food help us?

....

....

2. Name one food item we get from plants and one we get from animals.

....

....

3. Why should we not eat junk food very often?

....

....

Think Box

Find the names of these fruits in the word search.

strawberry

mango

apple

pear

tomato

orange

watermelon

R	S	D	L	E	W	S
M	A	N	G	O	A	T
D	O	P	I	G	T	R
Q	E	P	P	O	E	A
M	K	T	E	R	R	W
A	Z	O	A	A	M	B
P	I	M	R	N	E	E
P	G	A	R	G	L	R
L	C	T	T	E	O	R
E	O	O	A	U	N	Y

Life Skills and Values

A. Circle the food items you like.

1. 
2. 
3. 
4. 
5. 
6. 
7. 
8. 
9. 
10. 
11. 

Enjoy

A. Play this fun activity with your classmates with the help of your teacher.
Half a circle

Divide the class into four groups. Cut a few paper circles into halves. On one half, write a number. On the other half, write the same number in words. Exchange the half circle within your group. Now, move around the activity area by skipping, jogging, walking or hopping and trade the circles when you meet a classmate moving the same way. When you find the other half of your circle, only then can you stop.

B. On a sheet of paper, draw one special dish cooked for festivals like Diwali, Christmas and Eid.

Across the Boundary 2

Sandwich for Mother

Make a sandwich for Mummy and yourself. Write 1, 2, 3, 4, 5 and 6 in the boxes to put the pictures in the right order.

a.

b.

c.

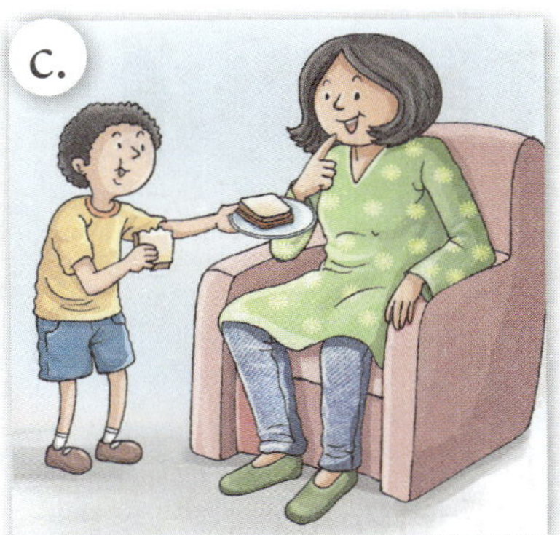

d.

e.

f.

6 Water

Let's learn about...

- uses of water.
- sources of water.
- ways of saving water.

Key Terms

- uses of water
- sources of water
- saving water
- storing water

Reflect

Which of these activities need water? Colour those boxes green.

Water is colourless. It is also tasteless and does not smell of anything. Water takes the shape of the container it is kept in.

FactPedia

Plants store a lot of water. Plants need water to produce food.

Uses of Water

We need water to live. Plants and animals also need water to live. We use water in many ways in our home. Water is used for activities, such as, drinking, bathing, cooking, washing and others.

drinking *bathing* *brushing*

having fun

cooking

cleaning

washing fruits

We use water for fun activities like swimming, painting and skiing.

Sources of water

We open taps and get water at home. Have you thought where does water come from in the pipes? Rainwater is the main source of water on Earth.

Other sources of water are rivers, ponds, lakes and seas. Most of these sources are filled by rainwater.

river

pond

sea

hand pump

a well

Hand pumps and wells are the main sources of groundwater. These are built by people and fill up when it rains.

Storage of Water

At home we store water in bottles, pots and buckets. The stored water is used for drinking, cooking and washing. Drinking water can be stored in jugs, earthen pots and bottles. Tanks are used to store a lot of water. Dams are built on rivers to store water.

Dam

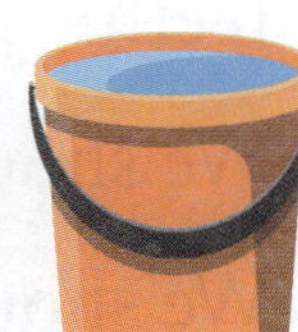
Bucket

Earthen pot

Bottle

skiing: to move over snow or water on skis; source: a place from where you get something; groundwater: water that is found under the ground; dam: A dam is a wall that is built across a river to stop the flowing water and to make a lake.

Clean Water

We should always drink clean water. Drinking dirty water can make us fall sick. Animals and birds also become sick if they drink dirty water.

We should never throw garbage into lakes, rivers and other sources of water.

Figure Out
How do you get clean drinking water at home?

DIY

Let us do two activities to find out about the qualities of water.

1. Take a glass of drinking water. See whether it has any smell or taste.
   You will see that clean water has no colour, taste or smell.
2. Pour the water from the glass into a small bowl. Does the water change its shape?
   You will see that water takes the shape of the container it is kept in.

Saving Water

Now, you know that water is useful to us in many ways. We must not waste water.

- We should close taps properly after use.
- We should not leave the tap running while brushing our teeth.
- We should take a bath using a bucket and not a shower.
- We should put used water into plants.

Close water taps properly

Green Earth
We can collect rainwater at home in big buckets and use it for watering plants in the garden.

garbage: waste items that we throw away

In a Nutshell

- Human beings, plants and animals need water to live.
- Water is useful to us in many ways.
- We get water from many sources.
- Rain is the main source of water.
- We should never waste water.

Workout

A. Fill in the blanks with correct answers.

1. We should .... (turn on/turn off) the taps after using them.
2. We should not drink .... (clean/dirty) water.
3. Water is .... (important/not important).
4. We can take out water from the ground with the help of .... (hand pumps/dams).
5. We need water for .... (cooking/reading).

B. Tick the activities that saves water.

1.  ☐

2.  ☐

3.  ☐

C. Answer these questions.

1. Name any two sources of water.

....

....

2. Write two ways in which you can save water.

....

....

3. How do you store water in your home?

....

....

4. Write any two uses of water.

....

....

D. Colour this picture.

Think Box

In groups, discuss what we can do to use water wisely and keep it clean. Write down the group's ideas and share them with other groups in the class.

Life Skills and Values

Do you know some people do not get clean water at home. They walk every day to nearby water sources to get it. They have to carry heavy buckets of water. Suggest one way to save water so that everyone has enough water to use.

Enjoy

A. Save Water Poster

In groups of five, make a poster for saving water. Your poster should have some simple steps to save water, a slogan and an interesting drawing that shows how we can save water.

B. Collect pictures showing the different sources of water. Paste them on a chart paper and display in class.

7 Our Houses

Let's learn about...

- the need for a house.
- the types of houses.
- the different rooms in a house.
- the different ways to keep a house clean.

Key Terms

- *pucca* house
- *kuchcha* house
- shelter
- parts of a house

Reflect

Complete these sentences.

- I go to my .... after school.
- When it rains, I go inside my ....
- I sleep in my ....

Need for a House

We live with our family in a house. A house is a place where we live and rest. It protects us from heat, cold and rain. It gives us shelter. It provides shelter to animals too. The house that we live in, with our family, is our home.

House provides shelter

Types of Houses

flats

Some houses are big. Some houses are small.

Tall buildings that have many houses in them are called flats.

Houses that are made of mud, bamboo and straw are called *kuchcha* houses. Houses that are made of bricks, cement and steel are called *pucca* houses.

kuchcha house *pucca house*

shelter: a place where we can live

Parts of a House

A house has different rooms for different activities. A living room to sit with guests. A dining room to have meals. A kitchen to cook food. A bedroom to sleep and a bathroom to bathe and wash.

kitchen

bedroom

dining room

living room

bathroom

Keeping the House Clean

- We should keep our homes neat and clean.
- We must open the windows to let fresh air and sunshine in.
- We should throw garbage into a dustbin. The dustbin should have a lid to keep flies and smell away.
- We should put our toys away after playing with them.
- Dirty clothes must be kept in a hamper.
- We should not write on the walls of our house.

Figure Out

What are people who build houses called?

DIY

Describe your house and draw its picture.

1. I live in .... (a flat/ own house)
2. My house has .... rooms.
3. The colour of my room is ....
4. I decorate my house with .... on my birthday.

hamper: a large basket with a lid to keep dirty clothes in

Decorating Houses

We can decorate our houses during festivals, weddings and special days. We decorate it with lights, flowers, rangoli, paintings, and other decorations.

FactPedia

In some places, people live in huge boats. These are called houseboats.

Green Earth

We should turn off the television, lights and geyser when they are not in use.

In a Nutshell

- A house protects us from heat, cold and rain.
- Some houses are big. Some are small.
- A house has different rooms for different activities.
- We should keep our homes neat and clean.

Workout

A. Fill in the blanks using words from the box.

neat	dining room	*pucca*	*kuchcha*	clean	home

1. A house is called a .... when we live with our family.
2. The two kinds of houses are .... and ....
3. A .... is a room used for eating meals with the family.
4. We should keep our homes .... and ....

rangoli: a traditional Indian art form using coloured sand or powder to decorate a floor or courtyard

B. Tick the activities you would do to keep your home clean.

1.

☐

2.

☐

3.

☐

4.

☐

C. Write the names of the rooms in which will you find these things.

1. bed ....
2. stove ....
3. study table ....
4. television ....
5. dining table ....
6. soap ....

D. Answer these questions.

1. Why do we need to stay in a house?

....

....

2. Name any two rooms of a house and their uses.

....

....

3. Write two ways in which you can keep your house clean.

....

....

Think Box

Imagine while going to your school, you saw few *kuchcha* houses where small kids were playing. How would that house be different from your house?

Life Skills and Values

We must help to keep our house neat and clean. Tick the items to find out if your room is clean.

1. Clothes or towels are on the floor.	☐	2. Dishes are in the bed room.	☐
3. Beds are made.	☐	4. Papers or books need to be put away.	☐
5. The floor is clean.	☐	6. Dustbin needs to be cleaned.	☐

Enjoy

A. Make a dustbin for your room.

You will need: a cardboard shoe box, wrapping sheets, glue, colours and stickers

- Take the box without the lid.
- Use glue to wrap a sheet around it. You can cover the inside of the box also to make it look neat.
- Your dustbin is ready. Decorate it as you want with colourful drawings and stickers.
- Place it near your study table.

B. Colour this picture.

Across the Boundary 3

Look at the untidy room. Clean the room by joining things to their proper places in the second picture. One has been done for you.

8 Clothes We Wear

Let's learn about...

- why we need clothes.
- the different clothes we wear in different seasons.
- why we wear uniforms.

Key Terms

- clothes
- cotton clothes
- silk
- taking care of clothes
- seasons
- woollen clothes
- uniform

Reflect

Look at these clothes and write their names.

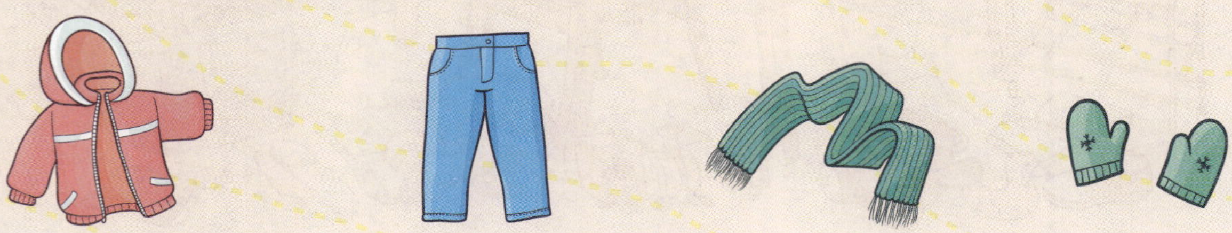

1. .... 2. .... 3. .... 4. ....

Need for Clothes

We wear clothes to cover our body.

Clothes also make us look good. They protect us from heat, cold and rain. They also keep us safe from insect bites, dust and dirt.

Types of Clothes

People wear various types of clothes in a family. Girls and boys wear different types of clothes. My father wears shirt and pant or kurta pajama. My mother wears a dress or a saree.

Summer clothes

Winter clothes

We wear different kinds of clothes during different seasons. We wear light cotton clothes when it is hot. Cotton clothes keep our body cool.

Green Earth
Some of our clothes are made from materials that come from plants.

Clothes in rainy season

We wear woollen clothes to keep our body warm. Woollen clothes are thick and are made of wool.

When it rains, we wear raincoats or carry an umbrella.

FactPedia
Sailors wear white uniforms and caps when they go to work.

We also wear rubber shoes called gumboots during the rainy season.

Special Clothes

We wear special dresses like lehenga for women and dhoti- kurta for men, on festivals and celebrations.

Sometimes people have to wear special clothes. These are called uniforms. People wear different uniforms to work. We also wear uniforms when we go to school.

Special clothes

Look at these people in uniforms. Name them.

....

DIY

Describe your school uniform by filling in the blanks. Then, paste a picture of yourself in your school uniform.

1. The colour of my shirt is ....
2. My school tie is .... in colour.
3. My (skirt/trousers) are .... in colour.
4. I wear .... socks to school.

Taking Care of the Clothes

We should take care of our clothes. We should keep them clean and dry. They should be washed regularly. We should keep them inside the cupboards neatly. We should not dirty our school uniform.

Wash clothes regularly

Figure Out

What kind of clothes does one wear while playing sports?

In a Nutshell

- Clothes protect us from heat, cold, rain and insect bites.
- We wear different clothes during different seasons.
- We keep special dresses for different occasions, like festivals and weddings.
- Special clothes that are worn to work are called uniforms.

Workout

A. Fill in the blanks.

1. We wear clothes to protect ourselves from .... and ....
2. Clothes are made up of .... and ....
3. Nurses, ... and .... wear uniforms to work.
4. .... and .... are worn to keep us dry during the rainy season.

B. Circle the correct names of these clothes and colour the pictures.

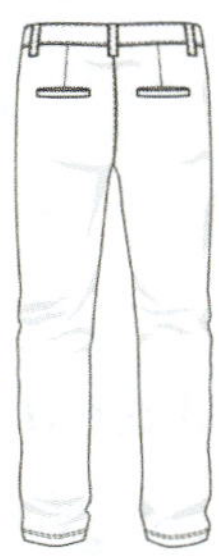

1. shorts/pants

2. shirt/trousers

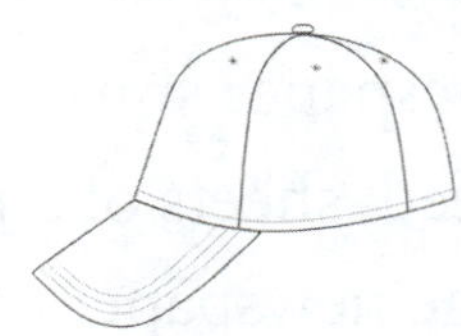

3. cap/scarf

C. Answer these questions.

1. Why do we wear clothes?

....

....

2. What type of clothes do we wear during summer?

....

....

3. How can we keep our clothes clean?

....

....

Think Box

How are clothes made? Name any three objects that a tailor uses to stitch clothes.

Life Skills and Values

What do you do with your old clothes? Tick the correct option.

1. Give them to a younger child in the family. ☐
2. Put them in a garbage bag to throw. ☐
3. Ask your parents to give them to charity. ☐
4. Give it to your helpers or their children. ☐

Enjoy

Make a newspaper shirt

You will need: sheets of a newspaper, a colour pen, a pair of scissors, and clear tape.

- Place one newspaper on top of another on a table.
- Draw the shirt on the newspaper with a colour pen.
- With the help of an elder, cut out the shirt. Make sure that you cut both the newspapers together. This will make both the front and back sides of the shirt.
- Using clear tape, stick the front and back sides of the shirt together.
- Your shirt is ready to wear. You can wear it for a costume party.

9 Air

Let's learn about...

- what air is.
- the uses of air.
- how air gets dirty.
- how we can get clean and fresh air.

Key Terms

- clean air
- space
- breeze
- wind
- weight
- storm

Reflect

What happens when we switch on a fan on a hot day?

- We can feel the air blowing. ☐
- The fan does not move. ☐

What is Air?

Air is all around us. Air has no colour and no smell. That is why we cannot see air but we can feel it. We feel air when leaves rustle and when a fan is switched on.

Air moves from one place to another. Moving air is called wind. When air moves softly, it is called a breeze. At times, the wind blows strongly. It is called a storm.

Breeze

Flying kite in the wind

Storm

rustle: the sound dry leaves make when they are moved

Features of Air

Why do balloons float? Balloons float in the air because they are filled with air. Air fills up the space around us.

Air has weight. A blown-up balloon is heavier than a flat one. Air occupies space.

FactPedia

When we blow air into water through a straw, bubbles are formed. Bubbles are balls of air in water.

DIY

Do this activity to know that air takes up space.

Pour water into a tub. Crush a piece of newspaper and push it to the bottom of a plastic cup. Turn the cup upside down and push it to the bottom of the tub. Now, pull out the cup and take out the newspaper. Check whether the newspaper is wet or dry.

The newspaper will be dry. This is because air filled up space inside the plastic cup and did not let the water in.

Uses of Air

Air helps us in many ways.

- Plants, animals and human beings need air to breathe.
- Footballs, tyres and balloons are filled with air.
- Air makes things fly.
- Air moves windmills and sailboats.
- Air dries wet clothes.

Air makes kite fly

Figure Out

How can we reduce the amount of smoke that goes into the air?

Air dries clothes

Air helps sailboat to move

Air moves a windmill

windmills: buildings with huge blades that move because of the wind; sailboats: boats that have huge sails that help them move

Pure Air

Growing a plant

Pure and clean air is very important. It keeps us healthy.

When we burn things, smoke is released into the air. Smoke that comes out of factories and vehicles makes the air impure. Burning dry leaves and wood releases smoke and pollutes the air. Dust also makes the air impure. If we breathe impure air, we may fall sick.

We need fresh air to stay healthy. Plants give out fresh air. We should plant more trees. We should walk or use a bicycle instead of a car to keep air clean.

Green Earth

Bursting crackers makes the air unhealthy for us. We must say no to crackers.

In a Nutshell

- Human beings, plants and animals need air to breathe.
- Air has no colour. It takes up space and has weight.
- Moving air is called wind.
- Smoke from factories, cars, crackers and burning leaves makes the air impure.
- We should plant more trees to get fresh air.

Workout

A. Circle the things that need air to move.

1. 
2. 
3. 
4. 
5. 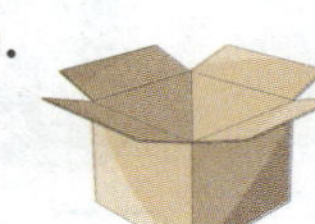
6. 
7. 
8. 
9. 
10. 

release: when something is set free; pollute: making the air or water dirty

B. Fill in the blanks using the words given in the box.

dirty	air	space	move

1. Leaves .... when the wind blows.
2. Burning dry leaves makes the air ....
3. Balloons burst when more .... is filled in to them.
4. When we fill air into a balloon it takes up ....

C. Answer these questions.

1. What is wind?

   ....

   ....

2. Write two ways in which air is useful to us.

   ....

   ....

3. How does air become impure?

   ....

   ....

Think Box

Tick the images which are not polluting the air.

1. 
☐

2. 
☐

3. 
☐

4. 
☐

Life Skills and Values

You know that planting trees would make air pure over a period of time.

Make a poster for growing more trees in your neighbourhood.

Write 'Plant Trees for Clean Air' below the drawing.

Enjoy

Deep Breathing Exercise

Let us do some deep breathing exercises. Find yourself a quiet place with a lot of trees. This breathing exercise is called bumblebee breath. Ask an elder to help you.

Steps

- Sit in a cross-legged position.
- Shut your ears with your fingers and close your eyes.
- Breathe in through your nose. Keep your mouth closed.
- Now, breathe out through your nose and start humming like a bumblebee.
- Repeat this twice.

10 Being Healthy

Let's learn about...

- healthy habits.
- keeping oneself clean.
- rest and exercise.
- the importance of keeping surroundings clean.

Key Terms

- habit
- cleanliness
- exercise
- indoor games
- outdoor games

Reflect

Circle the things you use to stay clean.

Healthy Habits

A habit is something that is done daily or often. The habit of keeping yourself clean is called cleanliness.

We should eat food that gives us energy and keeps our body fit. We should always drink clean water.

Figure Out

How do you feel in the morning when you do not get enough sleep at night?

Keeping Oneself Clean

To stay healthy, we must keep ourselves fit and clean. We should take care of our body. We must keep healthy habits.

We can keep ourselves clean in many ways.

FactPedia

If we do not keep ourselves clean, we might fall sick often.

Brush teeth daily

Wear clean clothes

Eat healthy food

Take a bath daily

Cycle to places

Exercise and Rest

Our body becomes strong if we exercise and take rest. Exercise keeps us fit and active. We must do some exercises daily to stay healthy. Stretching, jogging and cycling are some of the exercises that keep us strong and healthy. We should also do yoga, to keep our body fit and relaxed.

Our body also needs rest. We must go to bed early and wake up early.

Games and Health

Games that are played outside the house, like football, cricket are called outdoor games. Games that are played inside the house are called indoor games, like carrom, ludo and monopoly. Playing games is good for our health.

Playing together

Stay safe

We must follow healthy habits during a pandemic.

Wearing face mask

Washing hands with soap

Covering mouth and nose when sneezing

pandemic: an occurrence of a disease that affects many people over a very wide area

Keeping Our Surroundings Clean

We must keep our surroundings clean. Our body will be healthy when our surroundings are clean. We should always throw waste in dustbins, at home and in school. We should also keep our room neat and tidy.

Green Earth

Fresh air helps to be healthy. We should try to exercise in places that have fresh air.

In a Nutshell

- To stay healthy, we must keep ourselves clean and fit.
- We should exercise and take proper rest.
- We should play games.
- We should keep our surroundings clean.

Workout

A. Match the things that you use to stay clean with the body parts.

1. 
2. 
3. 
4. 

5. 

a. body b. nails c. clothes d. hair e. teeth

B. Fill in the blanks using the words given in the brackets.

1. To stay healthy, we must keep ourselves .... (dirty/clean) and .... (fit/unfit).
2. Stand .... (away/close) to the basin while washing your hands or mouth.
3. We should not .... (use/waste) water.
4. Our body needs .... (rest/no rest) and .... (no sleep/sleep) to stay healthy.

surroundings: the place where we live, everything around or near it

C. Answer these questions

1. Write two things you do to keep yourself clean.

....

....

2. What are indoor and outdoor games?

....

....

3. Why should we keep our surroundings clean?

....

....

Think Box

A. What do you think will happen if you only watch television and stop exercising?

B. We all follow clean habits. Colour the circle green for clean habits and red for unclean habits.

1. 

2. 

3. 

4. 

Life Skills and Values

Look at the pictures and follow the practice of washing hands to stay healthy.

1 *Water and soap* 2 *Palm to palm* 3 *Between fingers*

4 *Focus on thumbs* 5 *Back of hands* 6 *Focus on wrists*

Enjoy

A. Look at these different forms of exercise. Try to do these and tell your friends how you feel after doing them.

Cow pose Frog pose Camel pose Cat pose

B. Make a timetable of the activities you do daily. How much time do you spend playing games, doing exercise and resting?

11 Being Safe

Let's learn about...

- safety.
- ways to stay safe.
- good and bad touch.

Key Terms

- safety
- good touch
- first aid
- bad touch

Reflect

Look at these pictures. Circle the things you should never play with.

1. 
2. 
3. 
4. 
5. 

Safety means protecting ourselves from danger. We should always be careful and safe. We need to follow certain rules to avoid accidents.

Safety Rules

We should follow safety rules at all times and everywhere.

Safety at home

Do not play with sharp things

- Do not play with sharp objects, such as, scissors and knives. If you have to use a sharp object, ask elders to help you.
- Do not play with electrical switches and plugs.
- Do not open the door for strangers.
- Do not take medicine without the permission of elders or a doctor.
- Do not go near the heater, stove, oven or iron as they may burn you.

accidents: events that happen suddenly and result in an injury; stranger: someone you have never met before

- Do not play with matchsticks and candles or burn crackers alone.
- Climb stairs very carefully especially when they are wet.

Do not play with plug points

Safety on road

- Always walk on the footpath.
- Do not play or walk in the middle of the road.

Cross the road at zebra crossing

- Always cross the road at a zebra crossing.
- Before crossing the road, look to the right, then to the left and then right again. Cross only when the road is clear.
- Always hold the hand of your parent or an elder while crossing the road.

Walk on footpath

Traffic light

At some places on the road, we see traffic lights. The traffic lights tell the vehicles to move or stop. There are three colours in a traffic light— red, yellow and green. There are smaller traffic signals for the pedestrians. You can cross the road only when the pedestrian lights are green.

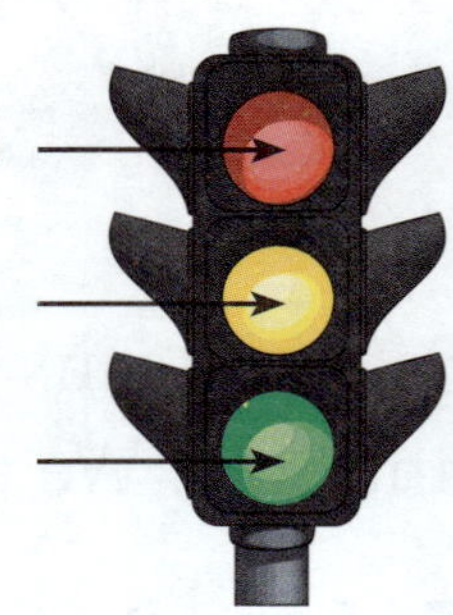

Traffic lights

DIY

Look at the things children do at home. Write Y for the correct action and N for the incorrect action.

1.  ☐

2.  ☐

3.  ☐

4.  ☐

footpath: a narrow path on the side of the road for walking; zebra crossing: black and white stripes at some places on the road; pedestrian: a person travelling on foot

Safety at school

Stand in a queue to board a bus

- We must follow some safety rules in class and at school too.
- Do not jump on desks and chairs. Do not sharpen pencil/s with a blade.
- Do not run about in the class or in the corridors.
- Do not push anyone while walking or climbing the stairs.
- Always stand in a queue while boarding and getting off a bus.
- In the playground, do not stand in front of swings or jump off the seesaws.
- While travelling in a bus or car, sit on your seat.
- Never put your arm or head out of the window. Do not disturb the driver.

Green Earth

One must avoid honking or blowing the horn of a vehicle again and again. It disturbs other drivers and creates unwanted noise.

First Aid

First aid is the first help given to someone who is hurt. We must keep a first aid kit at home, at school and in the car.

Good Touch and Bad Touch

Do you know a touch can be good or bad? Good touch comes from the people who love you. If your mother, father or your grandparents hug you before going to bed, it is a good touch.

good touch

Bad touch hurts your body or feelings. It is a bad touch if someone touches you where you do not want to be touched.

What you should do when someone touches you in a bad way?

- Say no. Tell the person that you do not like to be touched.
- Get away from the person whose touch you do not like.

- Tell your parents, grandparents, friends, teachers or any other elder person about this.
- Do not keep it a secret.

Figure Out

Who will you ask for help when your friend gets hurt while playing?

In a Nutshell

- We should always be careful and take care of ourselves.
- We should protect ourselves from danger and harm to avoid accidents.
- To be safe, we must follow certain rules.
- We should follow safety rules at home, on the road and at school.
- We must know about good touch and bad touch.

FactPedia

Zebra crossings have black and white stripes on the road, just like the stripes of zebra.

Workout

A. Write Y for the correct action and N for the incorrect action.

1. 

2. 

3. 

4. 

B. Write T for true and F for false.

1. We should always walk on a footpath. ....
2. We should cross the road when the traffic light is green. ....
3. We can stand in a moving bus and make noise. ....
4. We should not play with sharp objects. ....

C. Answer these questions.

1. Why do we follow safety rules?

....

....

2. Where should we walk on the road?

....

....

3. Write two safety rules that we should follow at home.

....

....

4. Colour the traffic light and write what each colour stands for.

Red ....

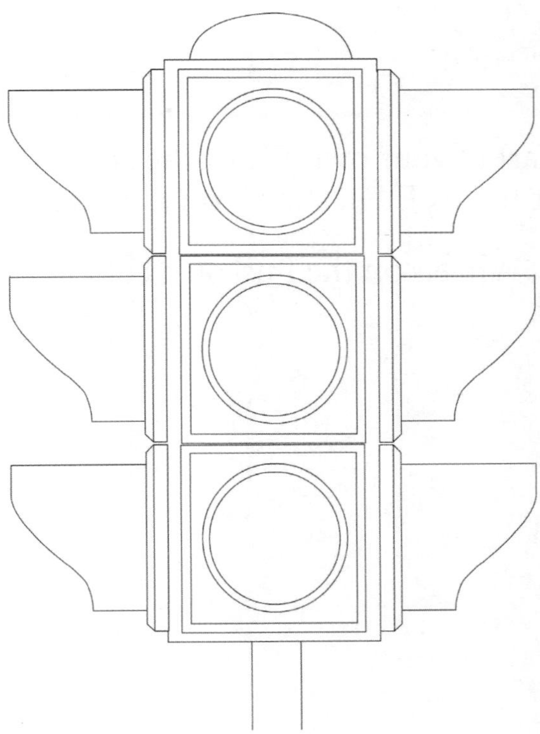

Yellow ....

Green ....

Think Box

What will you do if you see your classmates breaking the school rules? Tick the correct options.

1. keep quiet ☐
2. ask him/her not to break rules ☐
3. tell the teacher ☐

Life Skills and Values

Imagine you are walking towards your home from the park with two of your friends and a stranger calls you. Will you all stop to listen to him or keep walking fast towards your home?

Enjoy

A. Make a safety chart of your own. Draw the activities that you should not do at home and colour them. Then, stick it on the back of your bedroom door.

B. Write the rhyme 'Wheels on the Bus' on a coloured sheet. Sing the rhyme with actions.

Across the Boundary 4

Which of these things will you find in a first aid box? Draw a + sign inside the boxes next to those things.

1. 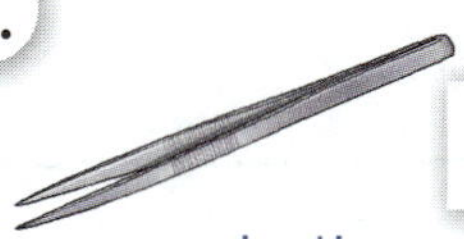
plastic tweezers

2. 

matchbox

3. 
bandages

4. 
paint

5. 
cotton swab

6. 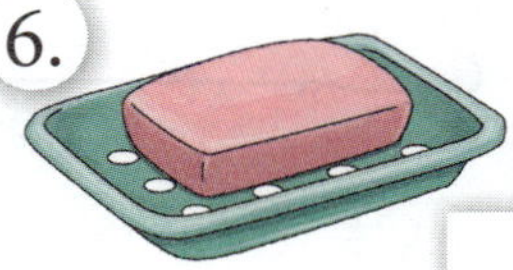
soap

7. 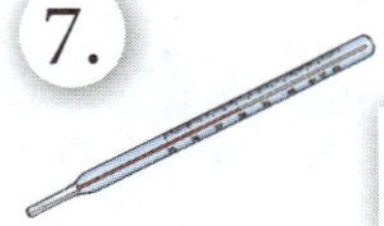
thermometer

8. 
hammer

9. 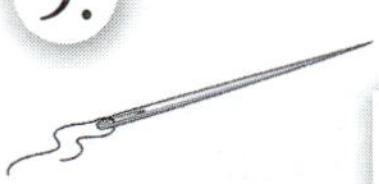
needle

10. 
disposable gloves

11. 
torch

12. 
toothbrush

13. 

antiseptic cream

14. 
antiseptic lotion

15. 
spade

12 Our Neighbourhood

Let's learn about...

- a neighbourhood.
- the places in our neighbourhood.
- respecting our neighbours.

Key Terms

- neighbourhood
- market
- fire station
- post office
- neighbours
- bank
- hospital
- respecting neighbours

Reflect

Where would these people go to get their work done?

- Gurpreet should buy apples from a ....
- Sohail wants to talk about his homework. He should speak to his ....

People who live near our house are called our neighbours. All the places that are found around our house form our neighbourhood.

A neighbourhood

Places in the Neighbourhood

A park

We see many places near our house, such as, park, school, hospital, post office and market.

We play in our neighbourhood park.

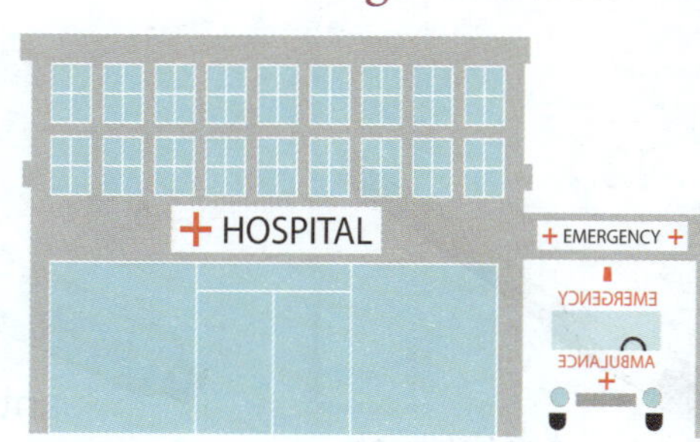

A hospital

Many people walk and jog in the park.

When we are ill we visit a doctor in a clinic or a hospital.

We send letters and cards to our relatives and friends from a post office.

A post office

A police station

A police station is a place where police officers work. Not every neighbourhood has a police station.

We also have a school in our neighbourhood. We learn many new things in a school.

A school

A market is a place with a grocery store, bakery and other shops, from where we can buy all the things that we need.

A bank is a place where we keep our money. A restaurant is a place where we eat.

A fire station

Fire stations are the places where firefighters are housed.

Some neighbourhoods also have a railway station and bus stops, from where we board a train and bus respectively.

Figure Out

Name two places in your neighbourhood.

DIY

Where in your neighbourhood will you find these things or people?

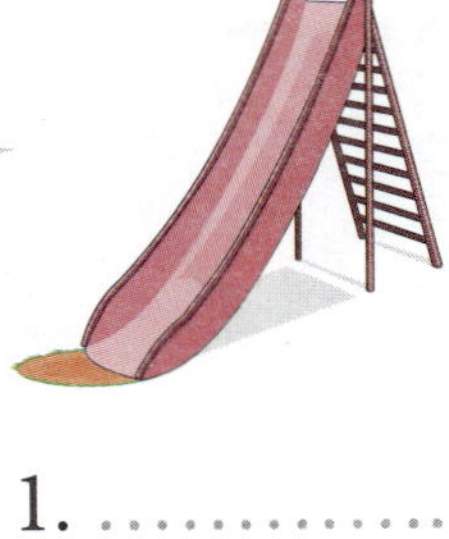

1. ....

2. ....

3. ....

4. ....

A Good Neighbourhood

When a family moves to a new house, they make sure that everything is close to the house. A good neighbourhood has all the places that we need. It is a place where people take care of one another.

- We should be friendly with our neighbours.
- We should help our neighbours.
- We should celebrate festivals with our neighbours.
- We should never fight with our neighbours.
- We should keep our neighbourhood clean.

FactPedia

A neighbourhood is also known as a colony. Ants and honeybees also live in colonies.

Green Earth

We should use dustbins to keep our neighbourhood clean. We should also plant more trees.

In a Nutshell

- People who live near our houses are our neighbours.
- The area around our house is called our neighbourhood.
- There are different places in a neighbourhood.
- We should help our neighbours and be friendly to them.

Workout

A. Fill in the blanks using the words given in the box.

park	neighbourhood	clinic	neighbours

1. A .... is the area around our house.
2. People who live in the same neighbourhood are called ....
3. We go to a .... to play and walk.
4. We go to a doctor's .... when we fall sick.

B. Match the places in the neighbourhood to the activities that are done there.

1. 

a. I go there to visit a doctor.

2. 

b. I can buy vegetables from this place.

3. 

c. I can take help from police officers in this place.

4. 

d. I can buy stamps from this place.

C. Answer these questions.

1. You have to send a letter to your cousin. Where will you go?

....

....

2. What is a good neighbourhood?

....

....

3. Write two ways in which you can be friendly with your neighbours.

....

....

Think Box

A. How do you help your neighbours? Write two ways in which you can help them.

B. Give two examples of the following:

1. Places in your neighbourhood used more often by people
2. Places in the neighbourhood used only when there is a need for them

Life Skills and Values

A. Ask your parents to help you remember the way to your house from the main road in your neighbourhood.

B. What will you do if you see someone not talking politely to a helper in your neighbourhood?

Enjoy

A. On a chart paper, draw a big circle or square to show your neighbourhood. Then draw small circles or squares to show places in your neighbourhood. Draw with a different colour places you would want to add to your neighbourhood.

B. Paste a picture of your best friend from the neighbourhood. Write two things about him/her.

13 People Who Help Us

Let's learn about...

- people who helps us.
- respecting people who help us.

Key Terms

- work
- respect
- people who help us
- community helpers

Reflect

Tick if you have seen these people working in your neighbourhood.

There are many people who help us in our daily lives. They help us with the things that we cannot do ourselves. They are our community helpers. You must have seen them working in your neighbourhood.

We must respect the people who help us. We must respect every kind of work. No work is big or small.

A paperboy delivers newspapers to our homes.

A milkman delivers milk to our homes.

A policeman keeps us safe.

A gardener looks after our garden.

A doctor treats sick people.

A farmer grows food.

A **teacher** teaches us at school.

A **tailor** stitches our clothes.

A **watchman** guards our houses.

A bus **conductor** helps the passengers and collects tickets.

A **nurse** takes care of us when we fall sick.

A bus **driver** drives the school bus.

FactPedia

A dentist helps us to take care of our teeth and keep them healthy.

Figure Out

What kind of work needs to be done at home?

Stay safe

We must respect and thank all our helpers, doctors, nurses, cleaners and police officers, who have taken care of the people affected by Corona virus disease in 2020.

DIY

Name the people that work in these buildings.

1. .... 2. .... 3. ....

In a Nutshell

- Different people do different kinds of work.
- Many people work to help us.
- We must respect all community helpers.

Green Earth

We must help the community helpers clean our surroundings by not throwing waste in public places.

Workout

A. Fill in the blanks using the words given in the box.

teacher	farmer	doctor	gardener	watchman

1. A .... treats sick people.
2. A .... makes our garden beautiful.
3. A .... grows food.
4. A .... teaches us.
5. A .... guards our houses.

B. Underline the correct option.

1. Ritu wants to buy a notebook and a pencil. Who should she go to? (milkman/ shopkeeper)
2. Amit's stomach is aching. Who should he go to? (greengrocer/doctor)
3. Shilpa's mother bought some cloth and she wants to get a dress stitched. Who should she go to? (tailor/police officer)

C. Answer these questions.

1. How does a milkman help us?

....

....

2. What work does a driver do?

....

....

3. Why should we respect all kinds of work?

....

....

Think Box

Solve these riddles and find out the names of some community helpers.

1. I fly a plane to help you travel to a different city or country.
   I am a P_ L _ _. (LITPO)
2. I bake tasty cakes and cookies for you.
   I am a B _ _ E R. (KABRE)
3. I help the doctor take care of you when you are sick.
   I am a N _ R _ _. (SUREN)
4. I deliver your cards, letters and parcels to your house.
   I am a P _ _ T _ A N. (PSOTNAM)
5. I look after safety of the people.
   I am the _ O _ _ C _. (PLCEOI)

Life Skills and Values

Respecting People Who Help Us

There are some children who cannot go to school. They have to work because no one else in their family earns money. Some of these children study on their own at home. We must help them because they work very hard. Discuss two ways to help these children.

Enjoy

A. Make a list of the people who help you at home, such as, the house helper, milkman, gardener, cook, guard and others. Take a chart paper and draw smiling faces on it. Colour them and cut them out with the help of an elder. Give these to the helpers to thank them for their help.

B. Make a list of the telephone numbers of the helpers who come to your home and paste it on the wall.

14 Plants Around Us

Let's learn about...

- plants in the surroundings.
- land and water plants.
- useful plants.
- edible parts of plants.
- care and concern for plants.

Key Terms

- trees
- shrubs
- herbs
- climbers
- creepers
- medicinal plants

Reflect

Look at these potted plants and answer the questions.

- Where do you find potted plants around you?
- Do you have plants in your home?

We can see plants all around us. We find them in gardens, in forests and even along the roads. Plants grow on land and in water. Trees and grass grow on land and lotus grows in water.

Plants in forests

Plants near our home

Plants growing in water

Types of Plants

Plants are of different shapes and sizes. Some are big and some are small. Big plants are known as trees. Mango, banyan and coconut are some examples of trees. Small plants are known as shrubs. Rose, hibiscus and tulsi are shrubs. Grapevine, and money plant are climbers which grow along a wall or fence. Small plants are known as herbs, such as, mint and coriander.

DIY

Look at the picture and name two types of plants.

....

Banyan

Rose

Grapevine

Coriander

Parts of a plant

A plant has many parts.

Look at the picture of a plant and read the names of its parts.

Figure Out

Which part of a plant makes food?

> **FactPedia**
> Plants make their own food with air, water, sunlight and soil.

Uses of Plants

Plants are very useful to us. Most of the food we eat comes from plants. We eat fruits, leaves, seeds, stem and roots of plants.

- Plants give us fruits and vegetables.

Fruits and vegetables

- We get food grains like rice and wheat from plants. We also get pulses like dal and gram from them.
- Some plants give us nuts like almonds and cashew nuts.
- Plants give us tea, coffee and sugar.
- Plants give us spices like cloves and cardamom and oils from seeds of plants.
- We get cotton, jute, rubber, paper and wood from plants.

nuts

Grains and pulses

Spices and oils

tea and sugar

- Plants also provide us medicines. Tulsi, neem, ginger and clove are medicinal plants.

Tulsi

cotton, paper and wood

> **FactPedia**
> Mango is the national fruit of India.

Taking Care of Plants

Plants make our surroundings green. We can sit under a tree to read or play. Many animals live on trees. We must not cut trees or harm them. We should take care of the plants by watering them regularly.

Reading under a tree

In a Nutshell

- Plants are all around us.
- Plants grow on land and in water.
- There are many types of plants.
- Plants give us fruits and vegetables.
- We should take care of plants.

Green Earth

We should not waste paper as it is made from trees.

Workout

A. Fill in the blanks with the correct answers.

1. Plants do not grow in ....

   a. forests b. water c. park d. boxes

2. We get .... from plants.

   a. meat b. fruit c. egg d. cake

3. Mint is the .... of a plant.

   a. leaf b. root c. flower d. stem

B. Name the following.

1. A plant that grows in water ....
2. A medicinal plant ....
3. A vegetable we eat ....
4. A fruit we eat ....

C. Answer these questions.

1. Where do plants grow?

   ....

   ....

2. Name any two parts of a plant.

3. Name three things that we get from plants.

Think Box

What will happen if a plant is not given water for two days?

Life Skills and Values

A. Imagine you are a plant and someone wants to adopt you. Write three things you would like your new owner to do for you.

B. If a tree is cut down, which of these will be affected by it?

a. Your pet dog ☐ b. Parrots ☐ c. Squirrels ☐

Enjoy

A. Make a plant friend.

Go to your neighbourhood park and choose a small plant you like. Find out its name by asking either a gardener or an adult. Take care of the plant by watering it daily with a bottle of water.

B. Draw a tree and colour it.

15 The World Of Animals

Let's learn about...

- animals in our surroundings.
- pets, wild and domestic animals.
- care and compassion for pet animals.
- common birds and animals in our surroundings.
- the sounds of some animals and birds.

Key Terms

- wild animals
- domestic animals
- pet animals
- farm animals
- birds

Reflect

Join the dots to draw a big and a small animal and colour them.

We see many animals around us. Some animals are big and some are small. We see birds, insects and fish too.

DIY

Look at the pictures of some common animals. Tick the animals you have seen.

1.  ☐
2.  ☐
3.  ☐
4.  ☐
5.  ☐
6.  ☐
7.  ☐
8.  ☐
9.  ☐
10.  ☐

Types of Animals

Some big animals live in forests. They are called wild animals.

Tiger

Lion

Koala bear

Animals that can be kept on farms or in our houses are called domestic animals.

We keep some domestic animals on farms. These are called farm animals. Farm animals help us in many ways. They give us milk, eggs and meat. They help to plough the land and carry load.

Cow

Hen

Goat

We keep some domestic animals at home. These are called pet animals.

Dog

Cat

Rabbit

plough: to dig and turn over land on a farm

Taking care of pet animals

Pet animals are our friends and are a part of our family. We should take care of them. We must keep them clean and give them food. If they are sick, we must take them to an animal doctor called a vet.

Keep your pet clean

Birds We See

We see many birds around us. Birds have wings and feathers. Wings help them to fly. Birds make different sounds.

Crow

Sparrow

Pigeon

FactPedia

Blue whale is the largest animal in the world.

Animal sounds

Animals and birds make different sounds. Some are given here.

Where do animals live

Most animals live on land. Many wild animals live in forests.

Lion

Zebra

Tiger

Green Earth

Many animals and birds live on trees. We should not cut trees as this destroys their home.

vet: a person whose job is to treat animals who are sick or injured

Some animals and birds live on trees.

Monkey

Squirrel

Figure Out

People keep fish in a bowl or glass box. What is it called?

Some animals like fish, turtle and dolphin live in water. Fish have fins to help them swim in water.

Fish

Frog

Crocodile

Some other animals like tortoise, frog and crocodiles can live both on land and in water.

In a Nutshell

- Animals are big and small.
- Wild animals live in forests or natural shelters like a cave.
- Domestic animals live on farms or in houses.
- Animals live on land, trees and in water.

Workout

A. Name these animals using the words given in the box.

deer   giraffe   camel   rhinoceros

1. 

....

2. 

....

3. 

....

4. 

....

B. Write the names of three pet, domestic and wild animals.

Pets	Domestic	Wild
....	....	....
....	....	....
....	....	....

C. Answer these questions.

1. What are wild animals?

    ....

    ....

2. What are domestic animals?

    ....

    ....

3. What are pet animals? Why do we need to look after them?

    ....

    ....

Think Box

Solve these riddles.

1. I am the king of the jungle. .... (OINL)
2. I have a long trunk. .... (LEEPAHTN)
3. I am the tallest animal in the jungle. .... (FFGRIAE)
4. I am the fastest animal. .... (AHCEETH)

Life Skills and Values

Visit a local wildlife park or a farm. Write four lines about the animal you liked the most. Write how it looks, the sound it makes and the type of food it eats. Draw or paste its picture in your notebook.

Enjoy

A. Make your own paper dog

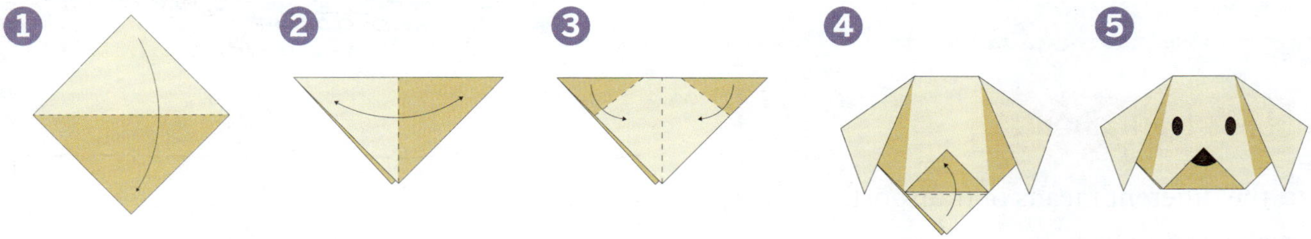

You will need one square paper, a black and a brown colour sketch pen.

1. Fold the square paper as shown in the step 1, 2, 3 and 4. Take help from your teacher or an elder person.
2. Draw the eyes and nose with a black pen.
3. Colour the ears brown. Your paper dog is ready.

B. Draw your favourite animal and a bird. Colour it and give it a name. Pin it up on the board.

16 How We Travel

Let's learn about...

- the different means of transport.
- parts of a car.
- emergency vehicles.
- harmful noise.

Key Terms

- travelling
- vehicles
- land transport
- air transport
- water transport
- means of transport
- emergency vehicles
- noise

Reflect

- How did you come to the school today?
- How do your parents reach their offices?
- How do people cross a river to go for work?

We go from one place to another. This is called travelling. To travel from one place to another we need means of transport. They take us from one place to another. We travel to school, to work, to the market or for vacations.

Fast and slow moving vehicles

We use different kinds of vehicles to travel. Vehicles can be fast or slow. A rickshaw, cycle and bullock cart are examples of slow-moving vehicles. A car, bus, train and metro and an aeroplane are examples of fast-moving vehicles.

Ways We Travel

There are three modes of transport—land transport, air transport and water transport.

Land transport

The means of transport that move on land are called land transport. Land transport is of two types—road and rail transport. Cars, bicycle, scooter, auto, truck, bus are all examples of road transport. They run on wheels.

Land transport

Trains are a means of rail transport. They move on the railway tracks. They carry many people and goods at the same time. They take people to different cities and far off places.

Train

Air transport

The means of transport that fly in the air is called air transport. Aeroplane and helicopter are some examples of air transport. Aeroplanes take us to far off places in a very short time.

Aeroplane

Helicopter

FactPedia
A yacht is a sailing boat with an engine. It also has rooms.

Water transport

The means of transport that sail on water are called water transport. They help us to travel across rivers and oceans. Ships and boats are some examples of water transport.

Figure Out
Find out what a raft is.

Ship

Emergency Vehicles

Vehicles that are used to respond to dangerous or emergency situations are called emergency vehicles.

An ambulance is used for taking sick or injured people to the hospital.

A fire engine carries firefighters and things that are used for putting out big fires.

Police vans are used by the police officers to reach the sites of crime.

Parts of a Vehicle

You have studied about the parts of our body and parts of a plant. Do you know a vehicle also has different parts? Look at the different parts of a vehicle.

Parts of a car

injured: a person who is hurt; crime: activities that involve breaking rules

DIY

Many people help us to travel safely. Write the names of these people who help us to travel.

1. 
2. 
3. 
4. 

....

Traffic and Noise

We should always follow the traffic lights while on the road. Red light indicates 'stop'. Yellow light indicates 'wait'. Green light indicates 'go'. A traffic police officer controls traffic and ensures that traffic rules are followed.

Green Earth

All vehicles run on fuel. Burning fuel makes the air, water and land dirty. We should use it wisely.

When too many vehicles blow their horns, it creates unwanted sounds called noise. Noise is very bad for health.

We should take care of our vehicles. We should keep them clean and not tear seat covers or dirty the car windows.

In a Nutshell

- We use vehicles to travel from one place to another.
- There are three means of transport—land transport, air transport and water transport.
- An ambulance, fire engine, and a police van are vehicles used during emergencies.
- Many people help us travel safely.

Workout

A. Match the vehicles to the means of transport.

1. 

2. 

3. 

a. air b. land c. water

B. Fill in the blanks.

1. A .... is a means of land transport.
2. A .... is used to take the sick and injured people to the hospital.
3. A .... is a means of water transport.
4. A .... controls the traffic on the roads.
5. Unwanted sounds are called.................... .

C. Answer these questions.

1. Why do we need transport?

....

....

2. What are the two types of land transport?

....

....

3. Why is noise bad for us?

....

....

Think Box

A. Most vehicles move on wheels.

1. How many wheels does a cycle or a motorcycle have? ....

2. How many wheels does a car have? ....

3. How many wheels does a bus or a truck have? ....

B. How do you think people travelled before vehicles were made?

Life Skills and Values

You and your friend in your neighbourhood go to the same school but you travel in different school vans. Do you think this is bad for the air? Discuss with your classmates why it is bad.

Hint: You have read about it in the chapter 'Air'.

Enjoy

Make your own sailboat.

You will need paper, a drinking straw, a round plastic lid and play dough.

1. Cut out a coloured sheet of paper in the shape of a triangle and decorate it.
2. Make three holes on its straight side. This would be your mast.
3. Take a drinking straw and weave it through the holes.
4. Now, take a round plastic lid and place a ball of play dough on it.
5. Fix the straw in the play dough and your sail boat is ready. The boat can also float in water.

Across the Boundary 5

Sana is new to her neighbourhood. She wants to go to the market. Help her trace the path from where she is standing to the market and then back through the park.

17 How We Communicate

Let's learn about...

- the means of communication.
- modern means of communication.

Key Terms

- means of communication
- newspapers
- mobile phones
- letter
- television
- fax
- email

Reflect

- How did you talk to your parents when you were a baby?
- How do you think animals or birds talk to each other?

Telling others about your thoughts, ideas or feelings is called communication. We communicate by speaking and writing. Signs and symbols are also used for communicating.

Means of Communication

Means of communication are the different ways that we use to communicate. Letters, emails and telephones are a few means of communication. A letter is a means of written communication. Letters have the address of the person to whom they are to be sent. Letters are posted in a letter box.

Posting a letter

symbols: a sign, number or a letter thats stands for something

We use telephones to communicate by speaking. Telephones are the fastest means of communication. Nowadays, people use mobile phones to communicate with one another from anywhere. They are also used to send text messages through short messaging service (SMS).

Telephones

Fax machine

A fax machine is used for sending important documents and papers to another machine quickly.

Figure Out
What type of phone is known as a smartphone?

To communicate with many people, we use newspapers, radio and television. Newspapers carry all the important news.

Newspaper

The radio is is used to listen to news and songs. It is also used to send messages to a large number of people.

Television

A television is used for watching TV shows, movies and news.
The Internet is a modern means of communication.
Email is a means of written communication sent using the Internet.

Laptop

We should always be polite and kind while communicating. We should always greet people who call us.

The means of communication make our lives easy but they can also be misused.

- Do not share any personal information on the Internet.

Green Earth
We should turn off televisions and computers when we are not using then This saves electricity.

- Do not talk rudely to anyone using any means of communication.
- Do not play with any means of communication else they may get damaged.

FactPedia
Traffic police officers use signs to tell the people driving on the road to stop or move.

DIY

Write the names of these objects.

1. .... 2. .... 3. .... 4. ....

In a Nutshell

- We communicate by speaking, writing and by using signs and symbols.
- Letters, telephones, mobile phones, newspapers, radio, television and the Internet are a few means of communication.
- Means of communication can also be misused.

Workout

A. Tick (✓) the suitable means of communication.

1. Bhanwi wants to tell her father about the grades she got in her exam. How should she tell him?

   a. Write in a newspaper ☐ b. Call him ☐

2. A storm is predicted for tomorrow. How can this information be communicated to people?

a. By calling everyone ☐ b. By announcing on the radio ☐

B. Match the columns.

Column A	Column B
1. 	a. used to send documents
2. 	b. used to send emails
3. 	c. used to send SMS
4. 	d. used to communicate with many people

C. Answer these questions.

1. What is communication?

....

....

2. How can we send messages to a large number of people?

....

....

3. How does traffic police communicate with us?

....

....

Think Box

How do you think animals communicate with each other?

Life Skills and Values

A. We should always be polite and kind while communicating. We should always greet people who call us. If someone calls for another member of the family you should ask them to hold the phone for a minute.

B. What will you do if you hear someone talking loudly on the phone in a public place?

Enjoy

A. Play Show and Tell game.

Each one of you bring your favourite toy or a book or a picture of your favourite cartoon character to school. Talk about it in class and tell your friends why do you like it.

B. Collect pictures of the various means of communication and paste them on a chart. Name them and pin them up on the bulletin board.

18 Sky We See

Let's learn about...

- the morning sky.
- the afternoon sky.
- the evening sky.
- the Sun, Moon, clouds and stars.

Key Terms

sky	morning	afternoon
evening	night	Sun
clouds	Moon	star

Reflect

Look at these drawings. Circle the objects you see in the sky.

What do you see when look up, above the trees in a park? The big open space above us is called the sky. The sky looks different at different times of the day.

When we wake up in the morning, we see the sunrise and the clouds. The sky appears blue in the morning.

Morning

The afternoon is the time when the Sun is high up in the sky. School gets over during the afternoon. We come back home and have lunch.

Afternoon

Evening

When the Sun sets, it is called evening. It begins to get dark in the evening. We go out to play in the park during this time.

The sky changes its colour at night and becomes dark. We sleep at night.

Night

In the Sky

We see a bright yellow Sun in the sky during the day. It rises in the morning and goes down in the evening.

Figure Out
Why do stars appear small?

We see white, fluffy clouds floating across the sky on a clear day. On a rainy day, the clouds appear gray or black.

At night, after sunset, we can see the Moon and the stars in the sky. The Moon looks like a white ball in the dark sky. The Moon changes its shape. Stars are the small and shining lights seen at night in the sky. They appear to twinkle in the sky.

Moon

fluffy: soft and light

DIY

Look at these pictures. Write whether you see them at night or during the day.

....

Green Earth

When we burn crackers, the air becomes dirty and we cannot see the stars clearly. We should not burn crackers.

FactPedia

Some stars are big and some are very small. The Sun is a huge star.

In a Nutshell

- The Sun rises in the morning.
- We see clouds and the Sun in the sky during the day.
- The Moon and stars are seen in the night sky.

Workout

A. Match the columns.

Column A	Column B
1. morning	a. fluffy
2. afternoon	b. twinkle
3. evening	c. sunrise
4. clouds	d. hot Sun
5. stars	e. sunset

B. Name the following.

1. The time when the Sun rises in the sky ....

2. The time when the Sun sets in the sky ....

3. The time when we see stars in the sky..

4. A white ball in the dark sky ....

C. Answer these questions.

1. What do you see in the sky in the morning?

....

....

2. When does the sky look gray?

....

....

3. What can you see in the night sky?

....

....

D. Colour the objects that you see in the sky.

Think Box

When do we see a rainbow in the sky?

Life Skills and Values

A. The Sun gives us heat and light. How can we use it to save electricity during the day?

B. Look at the Moon daily for one week. It changes its shape each day. Draw any two shapes of the Moon.

Enjoy

A. Make a stars-and-moon wall hanging!

1. Draw the Moon and stars on a sheet of paper. Cut them out and colour them.
2. Make a hole in each of them and pass a string through it.
3. Tie the opposite ends of the strings to a long stick.
4. Hang this stick on the wall.
5. Your wall hanging is ready.

B. Draw a rainbow and colour it. Put it up on the board.

19 Weather and Seasons

Let's learn about...

- weather.
- seasons.

Key Terms

- weather
- seasons
- foggy
- rainy
- sunny
- cloudy

Reflect

Colour the box red if you do the activity when it is hot, and colour it green if you do the activity when it is cold.

1.  ☐
2.  ☐
3.  ☐
4.  ☐

Weather changes every day. Some days are sunny, some are cloudy, some are foggy, some are rainy, some are windy and some are cold. Weather can also change many times in a single day. It may be hot in the morning and suddenly it may get cold in the evening. When the weather remains same for a long time, we call it a season.

Seasons

During the summer season it is very hot. The Sun shines brightly and the days are warm. We like to stay indoors near a fan or an air conditioner. We enjoy soft drinks, such as, lemonade and milkshakes in summer.

Summer

We also like to wear light clothes made of cotton. Cotton clothes keep our body cool.

The rainy season is also called monsoon season. Before it rains, the sky becomes cloudy as dark clouds cover the sky. We carry an umbrella or wear a raincoat and gumboots during this season. They protect us from rain. On cloudy days, the weather can be cold and windy.

Figure Out

Why do we wear sunglasses on a hot, sunny day?

Rainy season

Winter

Winter is the cold season. In some places, it snows during the winter. Sometimes the weather becomes foggy and dark. Days are very cold and nights are long. During winter, we like to sit near room heaters or fireplaces and enjoy the heat. We wear woollen clothes to keep our body warm. We like to have hot food and hot drinks, such as soup.

Tick your favourite season.

Spring ☐

Summer ☐

Autumn ☐

Winter ☐

foggy: sky covered by thick clouds; fireplaces: a place inside the house where wood can be burnt to get heat

DIY

What do we use in different seasons? Tick the odd one out.

1. a.  Hot soup ☐ b.  Ice cream ☐ c.  Sunglasses ☐

2. a.  Gumboots ☐ b. 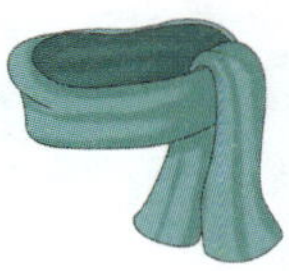 Muffler ☐ c.  Raincoat ☐

3. a.  Woollen cap ☐ b.  Juice ☐ c.  Coat ☐

FactPedia

Days are longer in summer season and shorter in winter season.

Green Earth

When the air is dirty, the weather changes and it gets hot.

In a Nutshell

- Weather changes every day.
- Weather can be sunny, cloudy, foggy, rainy, windy and cold.
- There are three main seasons—summer season, rainy season and winter season.
- We wear different clothes during different types of weather.

Workout

A. Identify the type of weather using the words given in the box.

cloudy	rainy	foggy	windy	sunny

1. 
2. 
3. 
4. 
5. 

....

B. Fill in the blanks.

1. Summer is the .... (hot/cold) season.
2. In winter, we wear .... (cotton/woollen) clothes.
3. Rainy season is also known as .... (summer/monsoon) season.
4. We wear .... (sweater/cotton clothes) in the summers.

C. Answer these questions.

1. What kind of weather is there during monsoon season?

....

....

2. Why do we like to stay indoors during summers?

....

....

3. What do we wear during the rainy season?

....

....

Think Box

Why do farmers worry when there is no rain for a long time?

Life Skills and Values

A. Let us learn how to make orange ice cubes for the summer season.

Steps

- Take 8 to 10 tablespoons of orange squash in a bowl and add 4 glasses of drinking water.
- Stir well and pour it into an ice tray.
- Put it in the freezer for 6 to 8 hours.
- Take out the tray.
- Your orange ice cubes are ready. Mix them with water and enjoy a cold and healthy juice in summers.

Enjoy

Join the numbers and colour the picture.

Test Yourself I

A. Write T for true and F for false.

1. We need food to live, grow and stay healthy. ....
2. *Kuchcha* houses are made of cement and bricks. ....
3. We have three meals in a day—breakfast, lunch and dinner. ....
4. Clothes cover our body and keep us warm. ....

B. Match the columns.

	Column A		Column B
1.	hobby	a.	outdoor game
2.	breathe	b.	mud and straw
3.	siblings	c.	done in free time
4.	hopscotch	d.	nose
5.	*kuchcha* house	e.	brothers and sisters

C. Identify the food items given below.

1. 
....

2. 
....

3. 
....

4. 
....

5. 

....

6. 
....

D. Label the rooms in a house.

....

....

....

....

....

Test Yourself II

A. Look at the pictures and write P for pet animals and F for farm animals.

1.  ☐
2.  ☐
3.  ☐
4.  ☐
5.  ☐
6.  ☐

B. List one safety rule you should follow at home, in school and on road each.

1. ....
2. ....
3. ....

C. Fill in the blanks using the words given in the help box.

safety	seven	colonies	domestic	pure

1. We must follow the .... rules on the road.
2. Ants and honey bees live in ....
3. Camels, horses and cows are .... animals.
4. We have .... days in a week.
5. We must drink .... water.

D. Write two sentences about the picture.

....

....

E. Look at the picture and label the parts of a plant.

1. ....
2. ....
3. ....
4. ....
5. ....
6. ....

Play the game 'Trek to your holiday home'. Roll the dice and use a button to move from one place to another. Follow the instructions.